Product Failure Lessons For Product Managers

Examples Of Products That Have Failed For Product Managers To Learn From

"Practical, proven examples of products that were not successful that will help you to avoid similar product disasters"

Dr. Jim Anderson

Published by:
Blue Elephant Consulting
Tampa, Florida

Copyright © 2013 by Dr. Jim Anderson

All rights reserved. No part of this book may be reproduced of transmitted in any form or by any means, electronic or mechanical, including photocopying, recording or by any information storage and retrieval system without written permission of the publisher, except for inclusion of brief quotations in a review.

Printed in the United States of America

Library of Congress Control Number: 2013956279

ISBN-13: 978-1494247317
ISBN-10: 1494247313

Warning – Disclaimer

The purpose of this book is to educate and entertain. This book does not promise or guarantee that anyone following the ideas, tips, suggestions, techniques or strategies will be successful. The author, publisher and distributor(s) shall have neither liability nor responsibility to anyone with respect to any loss or damage caused, or alleged to be caused, directly or indirectly by the information contained in this book.

Other Books By The Author

Product Management

- How To Have A Successful Product Manager Career: The Things That You Need To Be Doing TODAY In Order To Have A Successful Product Manager Career

- Product Manager Product Success: How to keep your product on track and make it become a success

- Communication Skills For Product Managers: The Communication Skills That Product Managers Need To Know How To Use In Order To Have A Successful Product

Public Speaking

- Secrets To Planning The Perfect Speech

- Secrets To Organizing The Perfect Speech: How to organize the best speech of your life!

CIO Skills

- CIO Business Skills: How CIOs can work effectively with the rest of the company!

- Managing Your CIO Career: Steps That CIOs Have To Take In Order To Have A Long And Successful Career

IT Manager Skills

- IT Manager Budgeting Skills

- IT Manager Career Secrets: Tips And Techniques That IT Managers Can Use In Order To Have A Successful Career

Negotiating

- Preparing For Your Next Negotiation: What You Need To Do BEFORE A Negotiation Starts In Order To Get The Best Possible Deal

- How To Open Your Next Negotiation: How To Start A Negotiation In Order To Get The Best Possible Outcome

Miscellaneous

- Power Distribution Unit (PDU) Secrets: What Everyone Who Works In A Data Center Needs To Know!

- Making The Jump: How To Land Your Dream Job When You Get Out Of College!

Acknowledgements

Any book like this one is the result of years of real-world work experience. In my over 25 years of working for 7 different firms, I have met countless fantastic people and I've been mentored by some truly exceptional ones. Although I've probably forgotten some of the people who made me the person that I am today, here is my attempt to finally give them the recognition that they so truly deserve:

- Thomas P. Anderson
- Art Puett
- Bobbi Marshall
- Bob Boggs

Dr. Jim Anderson

This book is dedicated to my wife Lori. None of this would have been possible without her love and support.

Thanks for the best 21 years of my life (so far)...!

Table Of Contents

WHAT CAN WE LEARN FROM PRODUCT FAILURES?............................8

ABOUT THE AUTHOR 10

CHAPTER 1: HOW DELL PRODUCT MANAGERS STOLE CHRISTMAS ...15

CHAPTER 2: WHAT PRODUCT MANAGERS CAN LEARN FROM A $100,000 MISTAKE 19

CHAPTER 3: NEW COKE: A PRODUCT MANAGER CAMPFIRE STORY..23

CHAPTER 4: PEPSI FUMBLES A GATORADE MAKEOVER: LESSONS FOR PRODUCT MANAGERS 27

CHAPTER 5: WHAT PRODUCT MANAGERS CAN LEARN FROM THE TROPICANA MISTAKE 31

CHAPTER 6: PRODUCT MANAGERS NEED NEW PRODUCT FLOP INSURANCE 34

CHAPTER 7: PRODUCT MANAGERS WANT TO KNOW: WHAT HAPPENED TO THE MICROSOFT KIN PHONES?..............................39

CHAPTER 8: FIRE SALE – WHAT HAPPENED TO CISCO'S FLIP CAMERA? 43

CHAPTER 9: ARE THE BLACKBERRY PRODUCT MANAGERS PLAYING BELOW THE RIM? 48

CHAPTER 10: PRODUCT MANAGEMENT FAILURE: GOOGLE'S MOTO X 53

CHAPTER 11: GREAT PRODUCT MANAGERS AREN'T AFRAID TO STUMBLE ON THE WAY TO THE TOP 57

CHAPTER 12: PRODUCT MANAGERS NEED TO LEARN HOW TO FAIL.61

What Can We Learn From Product Failures?

Product failures are never something that a product manager wants to talk about. We all live with the secret dread that someday the product that we are responsible might turn out to be a failure. When that happens, we all expect that we'll be asked to leave the company.

It turns out that we're all missing an important learning opportunity here. Products do fail and they end up failing for a wide range of different reasons. Every product failure is loaded with fantastic learning opportunities for product managers. We just need to take the time an open our eyes to see what we can learn from each failure.

Some of the biggest companies out there have suffered very public product failures. Talented product managers at companies like Coke, Dell, Pepsi, Cisco, and Microsoft have all done their best to bring a product to market with the hopes of having a runaway success only to fail. Given all of the resources that they had at their disposal, these failures are even more surprising.

As product managers we need to carefully study what happened in each of these cases. There are lessons here for us. The better that we can understand what went wrong at these well-funded and well-staffed firms the better chance we have of avoiding making the same mistakes.

Contained in this book are the tips and tricks that you are going to need in order to start to spot when a product is going to turn out to be a failure. As you read each chapter, take a moment to think about how you can start to use the information in your job immediately. I think that you are going to be both surprised and pleased with just how much this information is going to help you to avoid making the mistakes that have caused so many other products to fail!

For more information on what it takes to be a great product manager, check out my blog, The Accidental Product Manager, at:

www.TheAccidentalPM.com

Good luck!

- Dr. Jim Anderson

About The Author

I must confess that I never set out to be a product manager. When I went to school, I studied Computer Science and thought that I'd get a nice job programming and that would be that. Well, at least part of that plan worked out!

My first job was working for Boeing on their F/A-18 fighter jet program. I spent my days programming fighter jet software in assembly language and I loved it. The U.S. government decided to save some money and went looking for other countries to sell this plane to. This put me into an unfamiliar role: I started to meet with foreign military officials in order to explain what my product did.

Time moved on and so did I. I found myself working for Siemens, the big German telecommunications company. They were making phone switches and selling them to the seven U.S. phone companies. The problem was that the switches were too complicated. Customers couldn't tell the difference between one complicated phone switch from another complicated phone switch.

The Siemens sales folks were in a bind. They didn't know enough about how the switches worked to tell their customers why they should buy them. Siemens reached out into their engineering unit looking for anyone who could help the sales teams out. I put my hand up and overnight I became a product manager.

Since then I've spent over 20 years working as a product manager for both big companies and startups. This has given me an opportunity to do everything that a product manager does many, many times. I know what works as well as what doesn't work.

I now live in Tampa Florida where I spend my time managing my consulting business, Blue Elephant Consulting, teaching college courses at the University of South Florida, and traveling to work with companies like yours to share the knowledge that I have about how product managers can make their product be a success.

I'm always available to answer questions and I can be reached at:

Dr. Jim Anderson
Blue Elephant Consulting
Email: jim@BlueElephantConsulting.com
Facebook: http://goo.gl/1TVoK
Web: **www.BlueElephantConsulting.com**

"Unforgettable communication skills that will set your ideas free…"

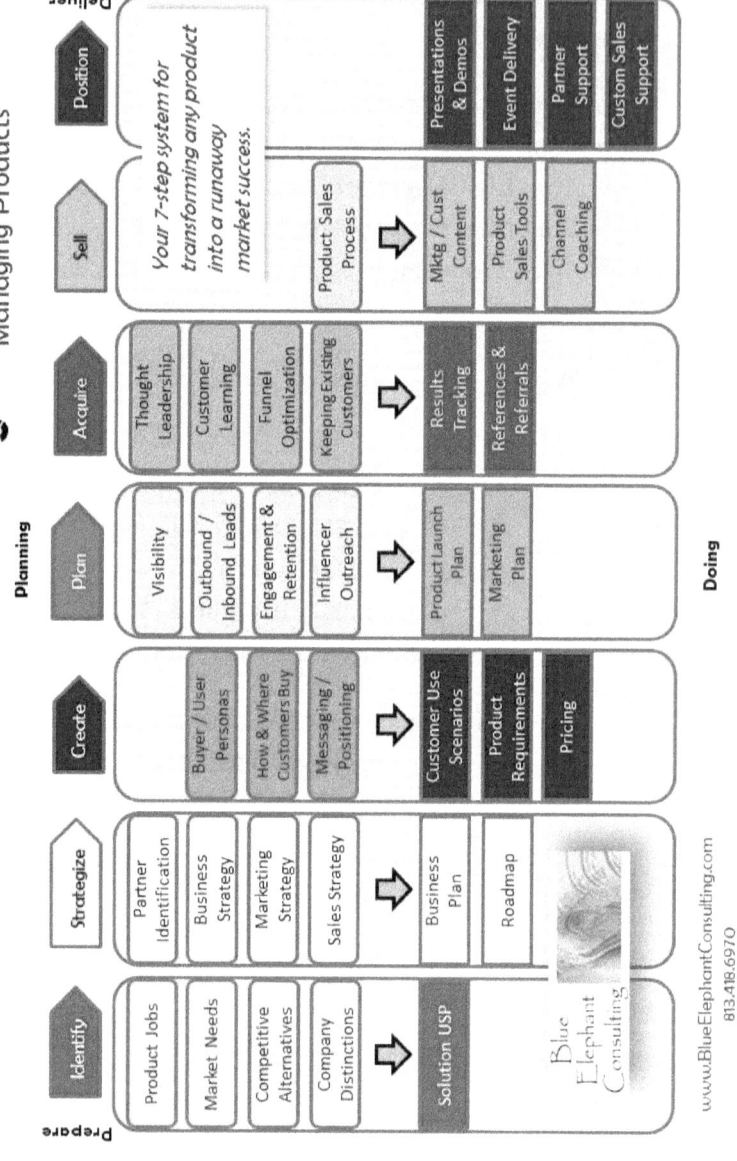

Create Products Your Customers Want At A Price That They Are Willing To Pay!

Dr. Jim Anderson is available to provide training and coaching on the two topics that are the most important to product managers everywhere: how do I create the products that my customers want and what should I price them at?

Dr. Anderson believes that in order to both learn and remember what he says, product managers need to laugh. Each one of his speeches is full of fun and humor so that what he says "sticks" with everyone.

Dr. Anderson's Product Management Training Includes:

1. How can you segment your market?
2. What problems are your customers having right now?
3. Which of your customer's problems does your product solve?
4. How much of this problem does your product solve?
5. How much will it cost your customer if they don't fix this problem?

Dr. Jim Anderson presents over 100 speeches per year. To invite Dr. Anderson to speak at your event, contact him at:

Phone: 813-418-6970 or
Email: jim@BlueElephantConsulting.com

Chapter 1

How Dell Product Managers Stole Christmas

Chapter 1: How Dell Product Managers Stole Christmas

Q: How can you tell when a Product Manager drops the ball?

A: When there is an article in the Wall Street Journal with the title "**As Holidays Approach, Dell Lags In New Products**"

Man, talk about having your failures broadcast to the whole world! In the consumer space in which Dell sells some of its PC and notebook computers, the end of the year Christmas holidays are the key to a company's survival. The sales that occur during this time generally account for 30% – 50% of Dell's annual consumer PC revenue. Miss this revenue train and you're going to be standing around waiting for the next opportunity for quite some time!

Where did product managers let Dell down? One place is in an ambitious mini MP3 player that Dell was planning on introducing. Way back in 2007, Dell bought a company called Zing in order to get access to their entertainment software. However, Dell then decided not to launch this product before the holidays a few years back. Ouch!

What this meant was that the folks who would have bought this product ended up going out and buying iPods and, maybe, Zunes. Once they did that, Dell was probably flat out of luck – once you've loaded your iPod up with $200 worth of songs, you sure don't want to change players.

Interestingly enough, Dell product managers were not just falling down in the cutting edge new product area, they also seem to be dropping the ball in their bread & butter areas such as notebooks. In this particular holiday season, Dell only released two netbooks (low end laptops, good for web surfing and emails) and some new paint schemes for some existing notebooks.

Remember, they are playing in a highly competitive market – Apple had just cranked out that very cool all aluminum Macbook and even Acer had released a bunch of new notebooks computers that had fancy styling and built-in access to 3G networks. What's was going on with those Dell product managers?

Michael Tatelman was Dell's retail chief. He had been forced to tell the press that *"You'll see some very sexy products coming out of Dell"*, though they may come out after the holidays. Double ouch!

Way back in the fall of that year, Michael Dell had told investors that Dell would *"focus on killer products…"* and they would have a *"shorter development cycle"* that would allow them to get products out "40% to 50% faster". Hmm, missing the Christmas season sure makes it seem like that didn't happen.

This wasn't the first time that the Consumer products division of Dell had missed a great opportunity. At the start of the school year they had to hold back on introducing their first netbook because of keyboard problems and so they missed most of the back-to-school selling window. That probably explains why the consumer products division failed to make a profit that year in the last quarter and why Dell ended up laying off 9,000 of its workers.

What's going on here? As product managers we are all probably quite familiar with the problems that Dell was facing. It sure looked like their new product pipeline, which is the lifeblood of Dell's consumer division, had a friction problem – products were not traveling through it quickly enough.

A product manager can't fix a problem like this by his / herself. However, it is our responsibility to get the various folks who can fix it together and knock some heads in order to get it solved. Since this problem had existed since the start of the school year, clearly there was a lingering sense of a lack of momentum at Dell.

What should the Dell product managers have been doing? They needed to start with a calendar to determine when they needed to have new products available in order to match up with their customer's buying cycles. Once they had this, then they needed to start with the finished product and work backwards.

What should the next product look like and what features will it have? Once this is nailed down, they need to determine how that product can be available by that date. Very basic stuff, but it sure looks like this was not happening. If a product can't meet a date, then you need to determine what functionally can be dropped to still meet the date. If too much would have to be dropped, then and only then should you start to move dates around.

Dell can recover from these blunders, but it's going to require that their Product Managers step up and take responsibility for fixing the system.

Chapter 2

What Product Managers Can Learn From A $100,000 Mistake

Chapter 2: What Product Managers Can Learn From A $100,000 Mistake

As product managers we are generally quite proud of our products. We do our best to work with potential customers and collect requirements. We ride herd over our developers to make sure that a good product is developed and that it rolls out smoothly. What happens if there is then a flaw in how the customer uses the product – are we at fault?

Kai Olsen from the University of Begen wrote an interesting piece that ended up in Computer magazine awhile back about such an incident. This story has a lot to teach us product managers.

It turns out that there was a very ordinary bank customer in Norway who used the Internet to do much of her banking. One day she wanted to transfer a large sum of money (roughly US$100,000) to her daughter. When she keyed in the daughter's account number during the transfer, she accidentally keyed in one digit too many.

This mistake resulted in the money being sent to an unknown third party who clearly thought that they had won the lottery. This third party promptly proceeded to gamble away much of the money before the police were able to step in and confiscate the remaining part.

Needless to say, this case got a lot of press in Norway. New banking regulations were requested to prevent this kind of slip up in the future. Obviously Internet banking had a lot more risk to it than most people thought.

In this case the end user was wrong – she entered too many digits. Before pressing enter, she could have corrected her error. At the same time, the system also could have caught and corrected her error. This did not happen – the team that built the system had not put such checks into the design.

The specific details around how this error occurred were as follows. The daughter's account number was 71581555022. The user entered 715815555022. The standard length of a Norwegian account number is only 11 digits so the incorrectly entered account number was truncated to 71581555502.

To make things even more amazing: the last digit in a bank account is a modulo-11 calculated number that should catch single key typing errors and cases in which two numbers have been interchanged. However, due to an unlucky coincidence the number that she typed was a valid account number.

Clearly the end user was very upset about what had happened. She took her case to the Norwegian Complaints Board for Consumers in Banking. She ended up losing her case – they said that she made the error and has to take the responsibility for it.

The user is taking the case to a higher court. She claims that since she typed in 12 digits, it was the responsibility of the system to give her an error message instead of just dropping all digits after the 11th.

As product managers we try our best to create high quality products that will serve our customers well. This case points out a clear failure of a product manager to do this job completely. What went wrong here?

How our customers interact with our product is, if not the most important part, than at least one of the most important parts of any product. Yes, we'd all like to have a very cool iPod / iPhone like interface that everyone raves about. However, even if we can't have that, it sure seems like it is a requirement that we have an interface that operates correctly and in a manner that won't harm our customers.

Chapter 3

New Coke: A Product Manager Campfire Story

Chapter 3: New Coke: A Product Manager Campfire Story

In the world of product managers there are a few stories that the old hands talk about when they get together. The product failures, the flubs, and the downright fiascos that have grown into legends that are now only mentioned in hushed tones when a product manager is trying to kill a product idea that he / she knows will doom a product. One such story is the tale of **New Coke**.

What Was New Coke?

You young whipper-snapper product managers out there might not be familiar with the story of New Coke, so we probably should go all the way back to **the beginning** – April 23, 1985.

The Coca-Cola Company had a problem back in the early 1980's: people were telling Coke that they liked **the sweeter taste of Pepsi** better than the taste of Coke. Being a careful company who didn't like to rush into anything, Coke spent the years from 1981 to 1984 taste testing both a new and the old formulas of Coke. They ended up doing this over **200,000** times in **25** different cities.

What Coke's Customers Told Them

The results of the taste tests were very clear to Coke's product managers: **55%** of the people tested preferred the taste of New Coke **over** the old formula. You might think that people made this selection because they didn't know what they were drinking. However, the product managers at Coke thought of this also – in the taste tests that they performed where the person knew which sample was New Coke and which was the old formula, people's preference for New Coke shot up by an additional **6%**!

What Happened When New Coke Was Introduced?

On April 23, 1985 Coke announced that they were going to **stop making Coke using the old formula** and from then on only make New Coke. Boom! The world blew up overnight – at least in terms of Coke drinkers. People overwhelmed Coke's customer support phone lines by calling to complain, they filed lawsuits to **stop the switchover** (which got dismissed), they said that they'd never buy Coke again, etc. Clearly the Coke product managers had made a huge mistake…

What Did Coke Do Wrong? (The Scarcity Principle)

So what did Coke do wrong here? Simple – they forgot about **The Scarcity Principle**. During those taste tests where people knew which sample was New Coke and which was the old formula, they also knew that they couldn't get New Coke at that time and so they naturally showed a stronger preference for **what they couldn't have**.

Coke probably thought that the 6% increase in desire for New Coke when people knew which sample was which meant that customers had a higher desire for something new. However, they were wrong.

When Coke replaced the old formula with New Coke, what happened is that people's desire for the old formula shot up because now it was **the thing that they could no longer have**. That's what caused the riots.

Final Thoughts

One of the best-supported findings in social science is that customers are **more sensitive to possible losses** than to possible gains. In this case, when Coke announced that they were going to stop making old formula Coke, this was a much bigger deal to Coke drinkers than the general availability of New Coke.

Product managers spend a lot of time listing out all of the benefits of their new products in the hopes of capturing new customers or getting existing customers to trade up. We all need to learn from the story of New Coke that sometimes our customers may **have become so attached to our existing product** that possibility of losing their existing product far outweighs the benefits of our new product. Being aware of this is how great product managers make their product(s) **fantastically successful**.

Chapter 4

Pepsi Fumbles A Gatorade Makeover: Lessons For Product Managers

Chapter 4: Pepsi Fumbles A Gatorade Makeover: Lessons For Product Managers

As a result of attending ProductCamp NYC I've been asked a lot more questions recently about how Product Managers can avoid making mistakes with their products. Half of that answer is to make sure that you understand the fundamentals of Product Management. The other half is **to learn from the mistakes of others**. Like the big mistake Pepsi made when they tried to change their Gatorade product...

The Problem With Gatorade

Pepsi's Gatorade story starts back in 2001 when Pepsi paid **$13.8B** to buy Quaker Oats and got Gatorade as part of the deal. Gatorade has gone on to become Pepsi's second biggest selling beverage product by volume (after Pepsi!) and is a key driver of Pepsi's North American profits.

Gatorade currently has about **75% of the sports drink market**. However this market segment is coming under pressure as a host of new competitors have shown up. These competitors include teas, juices, and enhanced brands of water. Pepsi is responsible for some of this competition because they have introduced the Propel and SoBe Lifewater brands.

Pepsi's Big Plan

Gatorade has started to **lose market share** due to increased competition – sales are starting to slide. Gatorade has lost 4.5% of the sports-drink market and volume has slipped 17.5% in the first six months of the year. Clearly something needed to be done.

What Pepsi decided to do was to rebrand their product in order to attract new customers. They did this by simplifying the product label to a **"G"**. They also rolled out a complete marketing campaign to TV, print, and online outlets that asked the question "What is G?". Those of you with long memories may remember that they also paid for a Superbowl commercial that revealed that "G" was really Gatorade.

What Went Wrong?

Perhaps a better question is what didn't go wrong? After the product makeover, customers complained that they were **confused** by the Gatorade "G" campaign. What Pepsi had done was to replace the Gatorade product name on the bottle with a big "G" and at the same time they shrunk the distinctive lightning bolt's size.

It's pretty clear that what Pepsi was trying to do here was to make Gatorade **"cool" once again**. However, it's also pretty clear that they have flubbed up. Pepsi has done the worst thing that you can do to a brand – they've confused their customers.

Final Thoughts

Indra Nooyi was the CEO of Pepsi which this change was made. Unfortunately, she was at the helm when Pepsi has made two major product stumbles: the Tropicana disaster and now the Gatorade failure. Somehow Pepsi product managers have lost touch with **their customers** and seem to be getting caught up in too many internal meetings where they convince themselves that they know what their customers want.

Somebody at Pepsi needs to take a step back and stop the product rebranding madness. What's been missing from the Gatorade campaign is a **true reason** for the makeover. The core audience for Gatorade remains the same – athletes who are hot. Pepsi product managers need to spend their time finding ways to once again make Gatorade the brand that gets chosen at the right time. If they can do this, then they will have once again have found out how great product managers make their product(s) **fantastically successful**.

Chapter 5

What Product Managers Can Learn From The Tropicana Mistake

Chapter 5: What Product Managers Can Learn From The Tropicana Mistake

In the world of product managers, there are some events that are only spoken about in hushed tones. Examples of product manager decisions that, when seen in the rear view mirror of time, just seem so very, very wrong that you wonder why the decision was ever made. Up until now the poster product for this kind of MAJOR screw-up has always been **new Coke**. However, someone has taken its place – Tropicana.

The Problem

The Tropicana company sells orange juice. They've got a big problem with their product: **you can't see the juice that you are buying**. It's pretty much the only prominent orange juice brand that is NOT sold in a transparent bottle.

The Solution

In order to solve this problem, Tropican reached to marketing and design guru Peter Arnell. Arnell has a long list of successful product designs to his credit including DKNY, Tommy Hilfiger and The Home Depot. He has an approach to branding that he calls PowerBranding that he has developed and uses with his customers. He's quite good at what he does.

For Topicana, Arnell added a **picture of a glass of orange juice** to the front of the carton. Now you could see the product. Sounds like a winner, eh?

The Fallout

Well, the new product packaging design went over like a lead balloon. The public was **outraged** - the Internet blew up with critics and not satisfied with just bashing the new design, folks also went after Arnell. What was up with this?

It turns out that Tropicana customers had some very deep associations with the way that the product looked. With the new design, something that had been so very familiar was all of a sudden **very strange**. There's no arguing that the new design was well thought out (new Coke was well thought out also), but the product manager had not asked customers the key question: is it ok if I change the design?

Lessons Learned

Not all products have this kind of bonding with their customers, but it's the **responsibility** of the product manager to check – you wouldn't want to become the next Tropicana-like disaster.

Chapter 6

Product Managers Need New Product Flop Insurance

Chapter 6: Product Managers Need New Product Flop Insurance

Is there any part of a product manager's job that is more exciting than being responsible for introducing a new product? For that matter, is there any experience that can be more nerve racking than introducing a new product? If only there was some way that we could take out "flop insurance" that would help to prevent our becoming known as the product manager who introduced the next "new Coke" disaster…

Why New Products Fail

In 2003 34,000 new products were introduced. 90% of them failed. In 2008 122,743 new products were introduced and the failure rate was about 80%. Those odds **don't look so good** for your next new product introduction, do they?

Dr. Rita Gunther McGrath has been studying the tools that companies use to plan for new product launches and she thinks that she knows what we've been doing wrong. It turns out that **we've been using the wrong tools**.

What's Wrong with the Way That We've Been Doing Things?

As any product manager who has spent any time working for a large firm knows, there is **no shortage** of tools available to help product managers plan for the introduction of a new product. It turns out that most of these tools no longer work correctly.

The problem is caused by the simple fact that things have changed. A lot. Most of the tools that are currently available to product managers are based on an assumption that what's happened in the past can be used to predict what will happen in the future. Now that most of the markets that we design new products for are **moving so quickly**, these assumptions are no longer valid.

Is There A Better Way To Plan For A New Product Launch?

Thankfully, yes there is a better way. Dr. McGrath proposes that we start to use what she calls "**discovery driven growth**". This approach is basically a plan for learning more as the launch process moves forward. The part that I like about this way of doing things is that it doesn't require the product manager to have a lot of analytical information at the start of the launch process. In my opinion that's a good idea simply because there generally isn't a lot of information available!

What Makes This Approach Different?

So in the graveyard of products that were bad ideas from the start (e.g. New Coke, Pets.com, etc.) **what went wrong?** These products had bright, smart product managers running the show and they created elaborate, beautiful plans that they followed to the letter when launching their products.

It turns out that they did **two things** wrong and these conspired to cause them to fail. The first was that they started with untested assumptions and then used them as facts on which they built their launch plans.

The second thing that they did wrong is that they built **a false reality** that blocked out the truth. They built products and then second generation products even as they launched advertising programs and invested in a great deal of expensive marketing. They did so much work that it all started to seem real to them, when in fact everything was built on some bad guesses about what the market really wanted.

What Is The Right Way To Launch A Product?

Dr. McGrath says that what we should do is to start any launch process by **writing down** what our assumptions are as we are creating the business plan. Overtime we'll forget what our assumptions are.

Next you need to **identify the milestones** that you'll be reaching as you get closer and closer to launching your new product. Once the milestones are known, you need to determine which of your assumptions you'll revisit at that milestone in order to determine if they are still valid.

The ultimate goal of this is to spot when any assumptions are found to be **no longer be valid** as early in the process as possible. You may end up killing the new product, but you'll save the company a lot of money.

What All Of This Means For You

Launching a new product is the **ultimate thrill** for a product manager. If successful it can make your career. Likewise, if it's a flop then there is a good chance that your career at your company may be over and done with.

One of the biggest problems that product managers face when launching new products is that the planning tools that we use are **out-of-date**. They assume that the future will be like the past, and that just ain't true anymore.

Using the discovery-driven growth approach allows product managers to document what their initial assumptions were and to **revisit them** during the launch process. This allows any fundamentally wrong assumptions to be detected as early as possible and corrective action (including killing the product) to be taken.

Launching a new product is never easy. However, this new approach to launch planning just might make it **turn out successful more often!**

Chapter 7

Product Managers Want To Know: What Happened To The Microsoft Kin Phones?

Chapter 7: Product Managers Want To Know: What Happened To The Microsoft Kin Phones?

Gone in 48 days. Ouch – that's got to be some sort of record. As product managers **we try to do all of the right things** when we're handed the responsibility of birthing a new product: determine what our customer's needs are, understand the competition, calculate costs and price points, and create clever tag lines and flashy graphics to capture our customer's imagination. Microsoft's product managers did all of this (and more), and yet the Kin One and Kin Two mobile phones from Microsoft got yanked off the market after a life of only 48 days. What happened here?

What The Kin Was Supposed To Be

Microsoft, the corporation, realizes that the mobile ecosystem is a very valuable place to be. They'd like to create products that would be **used by mobile users**. The Kin was supposed to be their entry into this environment and they were going to get there by winning over the kids with the very hip Kin phones.

According to the New York Times, Microsoft spent two years to develop the Kin phones and **spent a lot on the marketing** to promote them. The Kin phones were manufactured by Sharp for Microsoft, and available exclusively on Verizon Wireless.

The Microsoft product managers had decided that they wanted to target those mobile phone users who are **addicted to Web based social media sites**. You know, sites like Twitter and Facebook. This market includes teens and so in order to have a chance, the Kin phones needed to be seen as being "cool".

Clearly, **something bad happened**. Microsoft is not known for walking away from struggling products. Remember that everyone says that it takes three tries for Microsoft to get something right. However, this time they threw in the towel after only 48 days. Clearly this product was doomed from the beginning. What went wrong?

Why The Kin Failed

Every product manager knows that a product consists of many, many **moving parts**. For a product to be successful, these parts have to all line up. However, for a product to be as much of a failure as quickly as the Kin was, there has to be a whole bunch of things that go wrong.

Priya Ganapati over at Wired has taken a close look at the Kin event, and believes that we can understand what went wrong **if we dig deep enough**:

- **The Operating System Matters:** in a perfect world, what operating system a mobile phone uses wouldn't matter. However, we don't live in a perfect world and so it does matter. The Kin used a bastardized version of the new mobile Windows OS. This meant that nobody knew what to make of it and so they reacted by not buying it.

- **How Much Does That Cost?:** when you are targeting kids, you need to keep in mind that they don't all have tons of disposable cash. The data plan that you needed to have in order to use the Kin cost $70/month. Ouch! It turns out that was too much for the market to bear.

- **Yes, We Have No Bananas:** Microsoft decided to not allow the Kin to make use of either apps or games. The social networking services that the phone came with were all that you were going to be getting. Anyone who has an iPhone or a friend who has one knows that these days mobile phones are all about the apps. No apps meant no sales for the Kin.

- **Your Dad's Cell Phone:** if you are trying to capture the hearts and minds of kids, then your product had better be "buzz worthy". The Kin was not – other phones that kids could buy, like the Motorola Cliq or a HTC Hero, were way cooler.

What All Of This Means For You

Microsoft's product managers **simply didn't do their homework** when it came to the Kin. The idea of creating a phone to go after the admittedly huge youth and social networking segment of mobile phone users was a good idea, Microsoft's execution was not.

They didn't go wrong in any one area. Instead, they **dropped the ball in several different areas** including creating a confusing product, making it too expensive, not permitting it to use apps, and missing out on the "cool factor".

Just because the Kin didn't work doesn't mean that Microsoft can't succeed in this market segment. However, the Microsoft product managers **need to do a better job** of doing their homework and listening to what their customers really want next time around.

Chapter 8

Fire Sale – What Happened To Cisco's Flip Camera?

Chapter 8: Fire Sale – What Happened To Cisco's Flip Camera?

Dang it! This was supposed to be a story about a product success, not a product failure. Pure Digital created the low-end highly portable video camera market a few years back and then got bought out for **a half a billion U.S. dollars** by the networking giant Cisco. Cisco is stuffed with smart, bright product managers and they should have been able to boost this successful product into outer space. But they didn't and now the Flip video camera is going away, what happened?

Why I Loved The Flip Video Camera

So I'm willing to 'fess up – **I own a Flip video camera**. In fact, I so fell in love with this product that I bought one early on when it was still owned by Pure Digital. However, after a while of traveling around in my pocket all the time, the screen failed. I ended up getting a Kodak Zi8 to replace it in part because the Zi8 had a feature that the Flip never did – it had a jack that allowed it to be used with an external microphone.

I kept my eye on the Flip over time because I was still **seduced by its small size**. I never again bought one simply because it never really seemed to change – the Flip that is being offered today sure looks the same as the Flip that I bought several years ago. Sure, they've come out with an HD version and some pretty "skins" that allow you to personalize it, but that seems to be about it.

What Went Wrong Between Cisco And The Flip

Cisco is a smart company. They employ smart product managers. **Something went wrong here**. Brian Chen and

Chunka Mui have both taken a close look at what happened here, and it's not pretty.

It appears as though the reason that the Flip product line didn't do well under management by Cisco is due to **two preventable sets of conditions**: the Flip was a bad purchase decision for Cisco and then Cisco did a poor job of managing the product once they had it. The product line might have been able to survive one of these mistakes, but it couldn't overcome both of them.

The Wrong Decision

Cisco should not have purchased the Flip product line. Sure, at the time it seemed like a good idea. Cisco's John Chambers announced that Cisco was buying Pure Digital so that they could promote products that would create content that would drive the need for bigger networks – Cisco's core business.

However, what was missed in all of the glowing press releases was that Cisco bought Pure Digital not because they were in **a fantastic "adjacent market"**, but rather because Cisco's core business was slowing. Because of this mistake, Cisco found itself in a market that it really didn't know anything about – consumer electronics. The forces that drive this market are unlike those that drive Cisco's main enterprise networking market.

Additionally, Cisco thought that their brand name that conveys quality and innovation in the enterprise market would help to **sell more Flip video cameras**. It didn't. I, for one, don't associate Cisco with home products and would rather buy something from Sony or Apple before I'd buy something from Cisco. Finally, any thoughts that Cisco had about using the Flip product line to cross sell its other products was a pipe dream. People who are buying a US$100 video camera are not going to be the same people who buy a US$25,000 high-end router.

Bad Product Decisions

Did I mention that the Flip product line seemed to be **stuck in a time-warp**? In the fast moving field of consumer electronics, this is the worst thing that can happen. The Flip pretty much got mowed over by the arrival of smartphones: both Apple and Android products keep getting better and better every couple of months at doing what the Flip does.

The Cisco product managers could have saved the Flip. Just like the folks over at MySpace, they could have **specialized to save the ship from going down**. One way to do this would have been to work very hard to incorporate social networking features into the Flip. Just imagine if you could shoot a video of your dog barking a Christmas song and then hit a button and have it automatically uploaded to both YouTube and your Facebook account. But that never happened.

Finally, the product never moved on. There was never a compelling high-end Flip product that I saw in magazines that caused me to pause, and look longingly at (e.g. the iPad 2) thinking about **what I could do with it**. The Cisco product managers would have had to be careful here, but things like a good zoom lens, Wi-Fi connectivity, and maybe even an apps store just for the Flip would have done the trick. We'll never know...

What All Of This Means For You

When a company wants to **grow its bottom line**, purchasing another company to get a successful product sure seems like a simple way to make this happen. However, the ultra-successful Cisco has just proved that this can actually be a risky way to do things.

Their purchase of the Flip video camera product line was flawed in several ways. Although the product was hot when they bought it, the future was already **getting cloudy** as smartphones kept getting smarter and cheaper. The lack of any compelling high-end features or social networking tie-ins reduced consumer interest in carrying this extra electronic gadget. Finally, Cisco just didn't know that much about the consumer market that they were getting into.

In the end it all comes down to doing **the basic product manager homework** that we've all been taught to do. You need to take a look at the market and understand what need they are looking to fill. Then you need to take a look at your product and make some hard decisions as to how you are going to be able to fill that need better than anyone else. It cost Cisco over US$500M to learn this lesson, let's hope that the rest of us can learn from their mistake…

Chapter 9

Are The Blackberry Product Managers Playing Below The RIM?

Chapter 9: Are The Blackberry Product Managers Playing Below The RIM?

Come with me while we travel back in time, not far, just 5 years or so. Now that we're here, take a look around. What do you see? I bet you see just about all of those corporate folks **using their Blackberries to make calls and check email**. Poof! Now we're back in current times. Something has gone horribly wrong at the Blackberry parent company, RIM, and is it the fault of RIM's product managers?

Nothing Is Every Constant But Change

One of the problems that all product managers face is that if they own a market there is no place to go but down. Research In Motion (RIM) certainly **owned the market** for smartphones before the term had even been invented.

RIM had a great relationship with CIOs and enterprise IT staff. Everyone was buying Blackberry servers and installing them at their company. The RIM product managers would **meet with corporate IT teams** and based on what their needs were, the product roadmap for the Blackberry phones would be laid out.

All good things have to come to an end. This happened in the world of Blackberry about two years ago. That's when sales of Blackberry phones to consumers **overtook sales to corporate users**. This was caused by two events: corporate users have more options so they are buying a lot of non-Blackberry phones these days and more consumers are upgrading to smart phones and since they've seen all of the business users with their Blackberries, it seemed like a natural next step.

This change in their customer base wasn't part of the RIM product manager job description. It has caught the RIM product managers by surprise: **consumers behave very differently from business users**. What's even worse, consumers don't have any central IT department that RIM product managers can meet with to find out what should be on their product's roadmap.

Why Things Went Wrong At RIM

So just how did the wheels fall off of the wagon over at RIM? It basically has a lot to do with **product speed**. For you see, the world of corporate users moves much more slowly than the world of consumers who have more options does.

According to Phred Dvorak before they knew what was happening the RIM product managers found themselves behind schedule: they had **product delays** and a bunch of new products ended up being scheduled to hit the market at the same time.

This isn't all the fault of the RIM product managers. RIM had all sorts of **internal issues** going on. They were internally divided into separate consumer and enterprise divisions with separate account managers and business development managers. Oh, oh. These two groups did not see the world the same way and lots of disagreements ensued.

The guys who started RIM are very bright. CEO Mike Lazaridis is an engineer and it turns out (hold on, you know where this is going) he is still **intimately involved** in all of the technical and strategic decisions that are made about RIM products. Ouch – so much for delegation!

What RIM's Product Managers Need To Do To Save The Day

So is RIM a sinking ship that the product managers should be preparing to flee? No way, RIM **has great market share** and, if they take the right actions, this is just a bump in the road. There are three things that the RIM product managers need to do in order to get their products back on track.

The first is to accelerate their product development and release schedule. Hopefully this skill is on everyone's product manager resume. The consumer world moves fast and **only the fast will survive**. This may mean that there will need to be separate consumer and enterprise product lines. Or, even better, accelerate the enterprise product line also and RIM can impress their corporate customers.

Secondly, the RIM product managers need to change their thinking about **what makes their product desirable**. Enterprise buyers were members of the IT team and the technical characteristics of the RIM products was what they were looking for. Consumers care about completely different things.

The RIM product managers need to worry less about the security of their product's transmissions and more about making sure that users have access to and can play **"Angry Birds"** on their Blackberries. This is a big change and it's not going to come easy.

Finally, I hate to say it, but the RIM engineers need to **leave the planning table**. Yes, the engineers still have an important role to play, but it is no longer one of strategic management or deciding what goes on the product roadmap.

What All Of This Means For You

What's going on over at RIM is not all that unusual – I've seen this happen a hundred times. The market for their product **has changed on them** and they weren't paying attention and now they are trying to figure out what they need to do in order to adjust to the new world that they find themselves in.

That new world **moves a lot faster** than the enterprise-led world that RIM is used to. That means that RIM's product managers are going to have to adjust what goes onto their product roadmaps (more consumer focused features and fewer technical ones) and they are going to have to step up and wrest control of the product away from the engineers.

The good news is that **this is not a hopeless situation**. The bad news is that there is not much time in which to turn things around. The markets in which RIM competes move very quickly so they are going to have to implement these changes very quickly or risk having their customers hang up on them.

Chapter 10

Product Management Failure: Google's Moto X

Chapter 10: Product Management Failure: Google's Moto X

As you slave away at your product management job, you probably dream of how great it would be to work at some progressive company where (finally!) **your skills as a product manager would be truly appreciated**. Some company that understood the important role that we product managers play and who would give us the authority to make things happen. A company like, oh say, Google. How great would that look on your product manager resume? Well, not to burst your bubble or anything, but the recent release of the new Moto X cell phone by Motorola seems to indicate that even these guys haven't got the product management thing straight yet...

The Project: Moto X

So just exactly **what was the "Moto X" project?** It turns out that it was a very important product for Motorola. A while back Google made a surprise move and purchased Motorola. A few years ago, Motorola had been a leading manufacturer of consumer cell phones with their Razr, Droid, and StarTAC lines. However, they had fallen behind and consumers were no longer purchasing their phones.

Google's purchase of Motorola was seen as a daring gamble by the firm. For the first time they were going to **get into the business of manufacturing real products** instead of just being a service provider. The big question that everyone was asking was what would the next cell phone that Motorola created under the guidance of their new Google master look like?

That phone was the Moto X. Google spent US$13B to purchase Motorola, everyone expected great things from the next phone. Given that there was this much excitement and attention being paid to the Moto X project, you'd think that the product managers would have no problems **getting anything that they'd needed**, right? Turns out that you'd be wrong...

What Went Wrong In The Product Management Area

The stories that are starting to leak out about how the development and launch of the Moto X project went are starting to tell a tale that most product managers would easily recognize. One of the biggest issues had to do with **the Android operating system** that the phone uses. Developers of the phone were able to work closely with other parts of Google, but when they sought help from the Android team they often received no response, people who worked there said. Ouch!

Additionally, there were significant concerns on the team that the Chrome Web browser app (created by Google) **wouldn't be able to come preinstalled on the Moto X**, because developers couldn't get information they needed from Google as to how it would function on the device, said a person familiar with the project. This is a clear example of a failure to communicate.

Not having **a strong relationship** may have prevented Motorola from incorporating the latest version of Android, said two people familiar with the matter. Considering that the phone is being made by a division of Google, you would think that having access to the latest version of the phone's operating system would be a no-brainer part of the product development definition.

Finally, in the words of one Motorola employee "It's not like we were equally disadvantaged—we were more disadvantaged." Clearly, the Motorola employees felt that they had **less access** to the Google resources that they needed than people who worked at other firms did.

Clearly **this is a product manager failure**. These obvious communication issues needed to be worked out and worked out early on. Going up the management ladder to get issues resolved or getting on a plane and having a face-to-face meeting would have been two ways to make this happen. Yes, the product was launched, but it could have been so much better if only these issues had been resolved.

What This Means For You

It can be very easy to dream about how great life would be if only we worked at a different company. However, every so often we get reminded that **every company has its own set of product management challenges**. Google's release of their Moto X cell phone shows us that even they have their own set of issues no matter what it says on their product manager job description.

The team that was responsible for managing the Moto X product ran into **a set of classic product management challenges**: communication problems. Despite the high priority of the project, they struggled to get the attention of the people that they needed to talk with.

These problems could have been solved with stronger product managers. **There is no product problem that you can't resolve**, you just need to take the time to do it right! Learn from Google's mistakes and make sure that your product doesn't suffer from the same problems.

Chapter 11

Great Product Managers Aren't Afraid To Stumble On The Way To The Top

Chapter 11: Great Product Managers Aren't Afraid To Stumble On The Way To The Top

A quick question for you: **are you afraid to fail?** Would you be willing to take on responsibility for a product that might not be a success? I'm willing to bet that a lot of us would say "no" – our company's product managers who are perfect are rewarded while product managers who fail are kicked to the curb. Nowhere on the product manager job description is there a place where you can brag about how many times you've failed. However, I'm going to tell you that you're wrong – get ready to fail if you want to succeed.

How To Kill Your Product Management Career

In your job right now, what would happen to you if you failed? If the account manager and business development manager for your product didn't get to you first, then that end-of-year review would still be a tough one to sit through, right? Let's face it, failure is not something that is rewarded in our workplace and in fact it's something that **we all actively avoid** if we possibly can.

However, maybe we're just setting ourselves up for a much bigger career disaster. Can we all admit that **the world as we know it is changing**? Can you remember watching old-time movies where the hero would get a job at a company and then spend his or her entire career working there? We all know that those days are long gone.

Something else is changing also: our jobs. The job that you had when you started working may already be gone. The one that you're doing right now probably won't exist in what, 2, maybe 3 years from now. This all means that **you are going to have to**

change and change involves risk and along with risk comes the very real possibility that you are going to fail.

How To Become A Success By Failing

Well, that failing stuff doesn't sound like it's going to be any fun. But wait, **has anyone else ever failed?** Turns out that yes, in fact most successful people can look at their past and point to failures that helped them to get to where they are now.

The poster child for this kind of "good failure" would be Howard Schultz – the guy who founded **the Starbucks chain of coffee shops**. We all know and love the Starbucks store today, but when Howard first started it he really blew it. There were no chairs, he played lots of opera music, and his menu was in Italian. Clearly he realized that he had failed, quickly adjusted, and went on to become a big success.

You can do the same. Failure is actually a part of your product's overall strategic management. You need to **learn to make lots of small bets**. Some of these bets will pay off, and some won't. It's through what you learn from the failures that you'll be able to make tiny changes to your approach and try, try again.

If we keep doing things the same way that we've always been doing them, then we will eventually stagnate and then **we'll go into decline**. However, if you have the courage to start to fail and to learn from those failures, then the future contains limitless possibilities for both you and your career.

What All Of This Means For You

Product managers who are afraid to fail **will never become a true success**. Oh sure, they may do ok for a few years, but when things get really rough, they'll wash out.

If you are willing to adjust how you view failure, **your career can take off**. Sorry, there's still no place on a product manager resume to proudly list your failures. However, if you can start to look at failures as simply being learning experiences that are not to be feared, but are to be used to become a better product manager then you'll be able to grow and become better at what you do.

No, you can't be an idiot about this and do silly things that cause your product to fail, but if you try your hardest and your product still fails than **you will have learned what doesn't work**. The big deal is that it takes courage for you to be able to do this.

Product managers who are a success have to had failures in their past. It's from the forge of failure that the steel of success is formed. Learn how to make small bets so that **you can learn what works** and what doesn't. Do this well and you'll become a successful product manager.

Chapter 12

Product Managers Need To Learn How To Fail

Chapter 12: Product Managers Need To Learn How To Fail

How do you feel about failing at something? I'm willing to bet that you are just like the rest of us in that **you HATE to fail**. It turns out that if indeed this is the way that you feel, then perhaps you've been missing out on some great learning opportunities. Maybe I should explain myself...

Your Brain On Failure

Failure should probably be a part of the product development definition. Something that most of us have never spent any time thinking about is just **exactly how we react to failure when it hits us**. More importantly, how our brains react to failure when it shows up. Jonah Lehrer has been looking into this and has made some interesting discoveries.

It turns out that when we fail, two very important things go on inside of our heads. The first is that something called **error-related negativity (ERN)** which is triggered immediately after we realize that something that we've done has failed. We're talking about a signal that shows up 50 milliseconds after the realization that we've failed and there's not a darn thing that you can do about it – it's pretty much involuntary.

However, that's not all. There is another signal that our brain gets about 100-500 milliseconds after we realize that we've failed. This signal is called the **error positivity (Pe)** . We have some control over this signal: it happens when we start to pay attention to our failure and we spend time thinking about the results that have been produced.

The really smart scientists who study such things tell us that product managers who are able to have **a large initial ERN**

signal and a more constant Pe signal are the ones who are best able to learn from failures.

How To Use Failures To Become Better

All of this brain signal stuff is good to know, but what's a product manager to do with this new knowledge? It turns out that it all relates to **what kind of person you are**.

Scientists believe that the world of product managers is **divided into two groups**: those of us with fixed mindsets and those of us with growth mindsets. A fixed mindset means that we think that we are as good as we're going to get at this product management thing. Those of us with growth mindsets believe that we can become better product managers.

Knowing about those brain signals, the scientists have done some studies. What they've found is that product managers with **a growth mindset** were generating a much larger Pe signal and were therefore able to learn more from the failures that they had.

I can almost hear what you are saying right now: great, **how can I get this "growth mindset"?** It turns out that it might be easier to do than you might think.

Product managers who surround themselves with people who are always telling them how smart they are seem to fall into the fixed mindset camp. However, those of us who surround ourselves with people who **complement us on our individual efforts** fall into the growth mindset camp. Being recognized for individual accomplishments seems to make a product manager want to understand why they've failed and to do better the next time around.

What All Of This Means For You

Every product manager will fail sometime. There's nothing that we can do about this: it could be a product launch that goes flat, a successful product that runs into a wall, or a competitor that shows up and takes our market away from us. The end result is the same: **we've failed**. You might not be willing to put this kind of experience on your product manager resume, but if you've been a product manager for any length of time it's happened to you.

What's important is how we handle this failure. Studies have shown that we have **two reactions to failure**: the immediate reaction and the one that follows it. Product managers who are going to be the most successful have a stronger response when they detect a failure and they then take the time to learn from their failure.

Taking the time to treat each failure as **a unique learning experience** is what allows some product managers to get ahead. If they've taken the time to surround themselves with people who praise them for their efforts, then they'll be able to turn every failure into a way to become better. Since we know that we're going to fail, this sure seems like a good thing to do! Now that's something that you can add to your product manager job description.

It's from the forge of failure that the steel of success is formed.

Hard Work Does Not Guarantee Success, But Success Does Not Happen Without Hard Work.

- Dr. Jim Anderson

Create Products Your Customers Want At A Price That They Are Willing To Pay!

Dr. Jim Anderson is available to provide training and coaching on the two topics that are the most important to product managers everywhere: how do I create the products that my customers want and what should I price them at?

Dr. Anderson believes that in order to both learn and remember what he says, product managers need to laugh. Each one of his speeches is full of fun and humor so that what he says "sticks" with everyone.

Dr. Anderson's Product Management Training Includes:

6. How can you segment your market?
7. What problems are your customers having right now?
8. Which of your customer's problems does your product solve?
9. How much of this problem does your product solve?
10. How much will it cost your customer if they don't fix this problem?

Dr. Jim Anderson presents over 100 speeches per year. To invite Dr. Anderson to speak at your event, contact him at:

Phone: 813-418-6970 or
Email: jim@BlueElephantConsulting.com

Photo Credits:

Cover - By: PSParrot
http://www.flickr.com/photos/parkstreetparrot/

Chapter 1 - By: Dell Inc.
http://www.flickr.com/photos/dellphotos/

Chapter 2 - By: EP Technology
http://www.flickr.com/photos/ep_technology/

Chapter 3 - By: Mike Licht
http://www.flickr.com/photos/notionscapital/

Chapter 4 - By: Michael Chen
http://www.flickr.com/photos/fillmorephotography/

Chapter 5 - By: Martin Ringlein
http://www.flickr.com/photos/mringlein/

Chapter 6 - By: Kevin Galens
http://www.flickr.com/photos/kevygee/

Chapter 7 - By: Shekhar_Sahu
http://www.flickr.com/photos/shekharsahu/

Chapter 8 - By: Mack Male
http://www.flickr.com/photos/mastermaq/

Chapter 9 - By: Ninja M.
http://www.flickr.com/photos/a_ninjamonkey/

Chapter 10 - ByTinhte
http://www.tinhte.vn/

Chapter 11 - By: Michael K
http://www.flickr.com/photos/vasto/

Chapter 12 - By: Mykl Roventine
http://www.flickr.com/photos/myklroventine/

Examples Of Products That Have Failed For Product Managers To Learn From

> This book has been written with one goal in mind – to show you how to identify what can make a product fail. We're going to show you what how to detect when a failure starts to happen and how you can prevent your product from failing.
>
> **Let's Make Your Product A Success!**

What You'll Find Inside:

- **HOW DELL PRODUCT MANAGERS STOLE CHRISTMAS**
- **NEW COKE: A PRODUCT MANAGER CAMPFIRE STORY**
- **PEPSI FUMBLES A GATORADE MAKEOVER: LESSONS FOR PRODUCT MANAGERS**
- **FIRE SALE – WHAT HAPPENED TO CISCO'S FLIP CAMERA?**

Dr. Jim Anderson brings his 4 college degrees coupled with over 25 years of real-world experience to this book. He's managed products at some of the world's largest firms as well as at start-ups. He's going to show you what you need to do in order to make your career a success!

www.ingramcontent.com/pod-product-compliance
Lightning Source LLC
Chambersburg PA
CBHW071807170526
45167CB00003B/1208